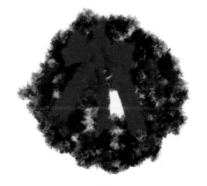

Presented to

_____

Given by

_____

The Joy of Christmas

A Potpourri of Holiday Stories, Poems, and Prayers

Compiled by Angela Kiesling

BARBOUR
PUBLISHING, INC.

Published by Barbour Publishing, Inc., P.O. Box 719, Uhrichsville, Ohio 44683
http://www.barbourbooks.com

Member of the
Evangelical Christian
Publishers Association

Printed in China.

The Joy of Christmas

A Potpourri of Holiday Stories, Poems, and Prayers

FRIENDSHIP
AND
SHARING

Lord, let me delight
in the gifts of loving friends
and a door to throw open wide
at this blessed time of year.
May I never take for granted those
who bring such joy to my life
and remind me, in so many
small ways, of You.
Amen.

The circle of our Christmas associations and the lessons that they bring, expands! Let us welcome every one of them and summon them to take their place by the Christmas hearth.

CHARLES DICKENS

Gentle, at home,
amid my friends I'll be
Like the high leaves
upon the holly tree.

Godey's Lady's Book, 1890

And they. . .breaking bread from house to house,
did eat their meat with gladness and singleness of heart.
ACTS 2:46

Back over the black mystery of old years, forward into the black mystery of years to come, shines ever more confident the golden kindliness of Christmas.

WINIFRED KIRKLAND

Now Christmas is come, let's beat up the drum.
And call all our neighbors together,
And when they appear,
Let us make them such cheer
As will keep out the wind and the weather.

WASHINGTON IRVING

He that is of a merry heart hath a continual feast.
PROVERBS 15:15

Scrooge was better than his word. He did it all, and infinitely more; and to Tiny Tim, who did not die, he was a second father. He became as good a friend, as good a master, and as good a man, as the good old city knew, or any other good old city, town, or borough, in the good old world. Some people laughed to see the alteration in him, but he let them laugh, and little heeded them; for he was wise enough to know that nothing ever happened on this globe, for good, at which some people did not have their fill of laughter in the outset; and knowing that such as these would be blind anyway, he thought it quite as well that they should wrinkle up their eyes in grins, as have the malady in less attractive forms. His own heart laughed: and that was quite enough for him. . . .

And it was always said of him, that he knew how to keep Christmas well, if any man alive possessed the knowledge. May that be truly said of us, and all of us! And so, as Tiny Tim observed, God bless us, every one!

CHARLES DICKENS,
A Christmas Carol

Sing hey! Sing hey!
For Christmas Day;
Twine mistletoe and holly,
For friendship flows
In winter snows,
And so let's all be jolly.

ENGLISH TRADITIONAL

May each be found thus as the year circles round,
With mirth and good humor each Christmas be crowned,
And may all who have plenty of riches in store
With their bountiful blessings make happy the poor;
For never as yet it was counted a crime,
To be merry and cheery at that happy time.

FROM AN EIGHTEENTH-CENTURY BROADSIDE

God bless the master of this house
Likewise the mistress, too.
May their barns be filled with wheat and corn,
And their hearts be always true.

A merry Christmas is our wish
Where'er we do appear,
To you a well-filled purse, a well-filled dish,
And a happy, bright New Year!

ENGLISH WASSAILERS' SONG

I'd like to be the sort of friend that you have been to me;
I'd like to be the help that you've been always glad to be;
I'd like to mean as much to you each minute of the day
As you have meant, old friend of mine, to me along the way.

I'd like to do the big things and the splendid things for you,
To brush the gray from out your skies and leave them only blue;
I'd like to say the kindly things that I so oft have heard,
And feel that I could rouse your soul the way that mine you've stirred.

I'd like to give you back the joy that you have given me,
Yet that were wishing you a need I hope will never be;
I'd like to make you feel as rich as I, who travel on
Undaunted in the darkest hours with you to lean upon.

I'm wishing at this Christmastime that I could but repay
A portion of the gladness that you've strewn along my way;
And could I have one wish this year, this only would it be:
I'd like to be the sort of friend that you have been to me.

EDGAR A. GUEST

13

M for the Music, merry and clear;
E for the Eve, the crown of the year;
R for the Romping of bright girls and boys;
R for the Reindeer that bring them the toys;
Y for the Yule log softly aglow.

C for the Cold of the sky and the snow;
H for the Hearth where they hang up the hose;
R for the Reel which the old folks propose;
I for the Icicles seen through the pane;
S for the Sleigh bells, with tinkling refrain;
T for the Tree with gifts all abloom;
M for the Mistletoe hung in the room;
A for the Anthems we all love to hear;
S for St. Nicholas–joy of the year!

FROM "ST. NICHOLAS," 1897

> At Christmas play
> and make good cheer,
> for Christmas comes but once a year.
> THOMAS TUSSER,
> *The Farmer's Daily Diet*

———⌒o

Catherine moved the conversation to something more cheerful. "What was your best Christmas?"

"My last Christmas with MaryAnne and Andrea. Andrea was at that age that she could sense the spirit of the holiday. Everything was tinsel and magic. Every bauble was for her. I felt it through her. That is the amazing gift of childhood." His words floated reminiscently. "How about you? What was your best Christmas?"

Catherine smiled thoughtfully. "The Christmas when I was nine. My family never had much. That Christmas I got a rag doll my mother had made from scraps she had saved from her sewing. My

oldest brother had brought home a pine, and we made our own decorations—painted walnut shells and paper snowflakes. I was so excited you would have thought that I had spent Christmas at the Vanderbilts'. Later on that day, my uncle, who lived just down the road from us, came to the house. He told my mother about a family whose father had been killed only two weeks earlier, leaving them destitute. My mother asked us children if we would be willing to share our Christmas. We all knew what that meant as we only had one present." She smiled. "There was a little flaxen-haired girl about my age. I'll never forget the look in her eyes as I gave her my doll."

David's eyes moistened as he considered the child's sacrifice. "That is truly remarkable, Catherine. What was your worst Christmas?"

A wry grin stole across her face. "Same one."

PAUL EVANS,
The Letter

HOME
AND
HEARTH

Sing we all merrily,
Christmas is here,
The day that we love best
Of days in the year.

Bring forth the holly,
The box, and the bay.
Deck out our cottage
For glad Christmas Day.

Sing we all merrily,
Draw 'round the fire,
Sister and brother,
Grandson and sire.

AUTHOR UNKNOWN

Christmas is here:
Winds whistle shrill,
Icy and chill,
Little care we:
Little we fear
Weather without,
Sheltered about
The Mahogany Tree.

WILLIAM MAKEPEACE THACKERAY

Christmas is coming,
The geese are getting fat,
  Please put a penny
  In the old man's hat.
    If you haven't got a penny,
    A ha'penny will do;
      If you haven't got
      a ha'penny,
        Then God bless you!

ENGLISH RHYME

Dear Father,
May the joy You have given me—
the joy You made possible
through Your Son's birth—
embrace those who enter this house.
I thank You for small things
and tender mercies.
Amen.

O Christmas tree, O Christmas tree,
Your beauty green will teach me
That hope and love will ever be
The way to joy and peace for me.
O Christmas tree, O Christmas tree,
Your beauty green will teach me!

TRADITIONAL GERMAN CAROL

The closet was full of Christmas. It smelled of dried pine needles, mothballs, crushed peppermint candy canes, and bayberry-scented candles. Bags overflowed with curlicued ribbons, paper chains, rolls of wrapping paper, and shiny strands of tinsel. Boxes of Christmas tree ornaments were piled in shaky stacks. They were waiting to be carried upstairs and dusted off, so they could shine in the light and work their Christmas magic again.

VALERIE TRIPP,
Molly's Surprise

Green grow'th the holly,
So doth the ivy;
Though winter blasts blow ne'er so high,
Green grow'th the holly.

Green grow'th the holly,
So doth the ivy;
The God of life can never die,
Hope! saith the holly.

ENGLISH VERSE, SIXTEENTH CENTURY

Dimmest and brightest month am I;
My short days end, my lengthening days begin;
What matters more or less sun in the sky,
When all is sun within?

CHRISTINA ROSSETTI

At Christmastime we deck the hall
With holly branches brave and tall,
With sturdy pine and hemlock bright,
And in the Yule log's dancing light
We tell old tales of field and fight
At Christmastime.

At Christmastime we pile the board
With flesh and fruit and vintage stored,
And 'mid the laughter and the glow
We tread a measure soft and slow,
And kiss beneath the mistletoe
At Christmastime.

ENGLISH TRADITIONAL

Hear the sledges with the bells–
Silver bells!
What a world of merriment their melody foretell!
How they tinkle, tinkle, tinkle,
In the icy air of night!
While the stars that oversprinkle
All the heavens seem to twinkle
With a crystalline delight;
Keeping time, time, time,
In a sort of runic rhyme,
To the tintinnabulation that so musically wells
From the bells, bells, bells, bells,
Bells, bells, bells–
From the jingling and the tinkling of the bells.

EDGAR ALLEN POE

M r. McAllister jumped up, opened the French windows and pushed the Christmas tree into the back garden. The next moment it went up in a great sheet of flame, and the McAllisters stood watching.

The tree burned steadily. Strands of tinsel shriveled and then became red-hot, glowing through the yellow flames. As they dropped to pieces, the glass baubles started to shatter. With high, musical pinging noises they exploded, spraying fragments of shining colored glass into the air: red, blue, silver, and gold in a steady shower.

Then it started to snow, white flakes floating down as the glittering, colored glass shot up. Where glass met snowflake, there was a soft hissing, audible over the steady crackle of the flames.

"Amazing!" murmured Stewart.

"Fabulous!" whispered Fiona.

"Terrible!" moaned Great-uncle Wilfred. He was still at the table, his face wretched. "I've ruined your Christmas. I'm a silly old man."

Fiona stared. "What are you talking about? It's marvelous. You've made my Christmas pudding wish come true."

"I have?" He blinked at her. "What was it?"

Fiona looked sheepish. "I wished we could have some flaming excitement this Christmas! But I never imagined an exploding Christmas tree bonfire. It's beautiful. Got any more ideas like that?"

"The Very Proper Christmas,"
The Oxford Christmas Book for Children

According to legend, mistletoe,
known as "the wood of the holy cross,"
was used to make the cross of Christ.
Afterward, in shame and anguish,
all mistletoe shrank to its present size.
Because of its supposed role in Christ's death,
mistletoe is never taken into a church.

Legend holds that holly came to represent the crown of thorns worn by Christ at His crucifixion. According to the legend, the holly berries were once white but turned blood red when the crown of thorns was pressed on His head. In Denmark, the name for holly is the Christ-thorn.

I can hardly describe the scene that met my sight. The room was brilliantly lit up with colored lamps hanging from the ceiling and the walls, and gaily festooned with green leaves and coronets of holly berries and mistletoe. There was no furniture in the room, but in the center, on the floor, there was placed a gigantic Christmas tree, whose topmost branches almost reached the ceiling. It was loaded with toys and presents, and dazzling with light which proceeded from a multitude of little tapers hung about among the dark fir branches in all directions. Little numerous glass globes, sparkling with various metallic colors that made them look like balls of gold and silver, added to the beautiful effect.

The company, especially the children, were astonished at the beauty of the Christmas tree, and were loud in its praises; and presently, some musicians in the next room striking up a merry tune, and all men, women, and children commenced searching about among the

branches for the toys and presents that bore their names. Such shouting and laughing, and singing and scrambling, and giggling and romping; such merry noise, and innocent, lighthearted gaiety; such joking, and quizzing, and bantering, as there was, as each one found the toy intended for him—I cannot describe for the life of me. I only know that for an hour or more the fun continued, till nearly every one in the room had possession of a bonbon in gilt paper, or a toy watch, or a box of crackers, or something of that kind. There were sugar-frosted fruits and sweetmeats, with mottoes slyly concealed inside, for the ladies and gentlemen; and little dolls, and little tops, and little colored balls, and all kinds of toys and confectionery for the boys and girls, with numerous other things for which I can find no names. And the romps grew loud and gay as the minutes passed.

"A Victorian Christmas Tree,"
The Oxford Christmas Book for Children

Wonder
and
Mystery

Gracious Lord,
I marvel that You came to Earth at all,
willing to leave Your royal abode
for a lowly stall—and a lowly life.
Let me never lose a sense
of childlike wonder
at this most blessed season.
Continually remind me that
You still work miracles
every day of the year.
Amen.

And there were in the same country
shepherds abiding in the field,
keeping watch over their flock by night.
And, lo, the angel of the Lord came upon them,
and the glory of the Lord shone round about them:
and they were sore afraid.
And the angel said unto them, Fear not: for, behold,
I bring you good tidings of great joy, which shall be to all people.
For unto you is born this day in the city of David a Saviour,
which is Christ the Lord. And this shall be a sign unto you;
Ye shall find the babe wrapped in swaddling clothes,
lying in a manger. And suddenly there was with the angel
a multitude of the heavenly host praising God, and saying,
Glory to God in the highest,
and on earth peace, good will toward men.
LUKE 2:8–14

In the bleak midwinter
Frosty wind made moan,
Earth stood hard as iron,
Water like a stone;
Snow had fallen, snow on snow,
Snow on snow,
In the bleak midwinter
Long ago.

Our God, Heaven cannot hold him
Nor Earth sustain;
Heaven and Earth shall flee away
When He comes to reign;
In the bleak midwinter
A stable-place sufficed
The Lord God Almighty
Jesus Christ.

CHRISTINA ROSSETTI

As if led by an invisible hand, the three camels pricked up their ears, raised their heads and went on toward the desert. Silence descended upon the group again. Above them the blue sky and all around them the sand, hot like fire under the rays of the sun. The magi looked at each other in silence and set their eyes on the road.

Darkness soon closed in. On and on the camels went. They could hardly see themselves in the darkness that enveloped them.

Suddenly, a star appeared large and resplendent, way up in the sky. Its light shone like a silver thread on the sand. In great silence, the three magi raised their heads to the sky and gazed long at the star. There was hope and faith in the three eager faces that now bent their heads to lead the camels on.

From somewhere a sound of bells was heard, faintly at first, then louder and louder.

"God be praised," said King Baltazar, "we are near the city. . . ."

PURA BELPRE,
The Three Magi

Enough for Him, whom cherubim
Worship night and day,
A breast full of milk
And a manger full of hay;
Enough for Him, whom angels
Fall down before,
The ox and ass and camel
Which adore.

Angels and archangels
May have gathered there,
Cherubim and seraphim
Thronged the air;
But only His mother
In her maiden bliss
Worshipped the Beloved
With a kiss.

Jesus, our brother, strong and good,
Was humbly born in a stable rude;
And the friendly beasts around Him stood,
Jesus, our brother, strong and good.

"I," said the sheep with curly horn,
"I gave Him my wool for His blanket warm.
"He wore my coat on Christmas morn,
"I," said the sheep with curly horn.

"I," said the dove from rafters high.
"I cooed Him to sleep so He would not cry,
"We cooed Him to sleep, my mate and I;
"I," said the dove from rafters high.

"I," said the cow, all white and red.
"I gave Him my manger for His bed;
"I gave Him my hay to pillow His head;
"I," said the cow, all white and red.

"I," said the donkey, shaggy and brown.
"I carried His mother uphill and down;
"I carried her safely to Bethlehem town,
"I," said the donkey, shaggy and brown.

And every beast, by some good spell,
In the stable dark was glad to tell,
Of the gift he gave Emmanuel,
The gift he gave Emmanuel.

ENGLISH CAROL

The Kings they came from out the South,
All dressed in ermine fine:
They bore Him gold and chrysoprase,
And gifts of precious wine.

The Shepherds came from out the North,
Their coats were brown and old:
They brought Him little newborn lambs—
They had not any gold.

The Wise Men came from out the East,
And they were wrapped in white:
The star that led them all the way
Did glorify the night.

The Angels came from heaven high,
And they were clad with wings:
And lo they brought a joyful song
The host of heaven sings.

The Kings they knocked upon the door,
The Wise Men entered in,
The Shepherds followed after them
To hear the song begin.

The Angels sang through the night
Until the rising sun,
But little Jesus fell asleep
Before the song was done.

SARA TEASDALE

What can I give Him
Poor as I am?
If I were a shepherd
I would bring a lamb,
If I were a Wise Man
I would do my part–
Yet what I can I give Him,
Give my heart.

CHRISTINA ROSSETTI

We have heard the children say–
Gentle children, whom we love–
Long ago on Christmas Day,
Came a message from above.
Still, as Christmastide comes 'round,
They remember it again–
Echo still the joyful sound,
"Peace on Earth, good will to men!"

LEWIS CARROLL

Oh, Mary, what you gonna name
That pretty little baby?
Glory, glory, glory
To the newborn King!

Some will call Him one thing,
But I think I'll call Him Jesus.
Glory, glory, glory
To the newborn King!

Some will call Him one thing,
But I think I'll say Emmanuel.
Glory, glory, glory
To the newborn King!

SPIRITUAL

'Twas in the moon of wintertime when all
the birds had fled.
That mighty Gitchi Manitou sent angel choirs instead.
Before their light the stars grew dim, and
wand'ring hunters heard the hymn:
"Jesus, your King, is born; Jesus is born: in excelsis gloria!"

Within a lodge of broken bark the tender Babe was found,
A ragged robe of rabbit skin enwrapped His beauty round.
And as the hunter braves drew nigh, the
angels' song rang loud and high;
"Jesus, your King, is born; Jesus is born: in excelsis gloria!"

The earliest moon of wintertime is not so round and fair
as was the ring of glory on the helpless infant there.
And Chiefs from far before Him knelt with gifts
of fox and beaver pelt.
"Jesus, your King, is born; Jesus is born: in excelsis gloria!"

Oh children of the forest free, oh sons of Manitou,
the Holy Child of Earth and heaven is born
today for you.
Come kneel before the radiant Boy, who brings you
beauty, peace, and joy.
"Jesus, your King, is born; Jesus is born: in excelsis gloria!"

"JESUS AHATONHIA" (JESUS IS BORN)
FATHER JEAN DE BREFEUF,
TRANSLATED FROM THE HURON LANGUAGE

Sweet dreams, form a shade
O'er my lovely infant's head;
Sweet dreams of pleasant streams
By happy, silent, moony beams.

Sweet sleep, with soft down
Weave thy brows an infant crown.
Sweet sleep, Angel mild,
Hover o'er my happy child.

Sweet smiles, in the night
Hover over my delight;
Sweet smiles, mother's smiles,
All the livelong night beguiles.

Sweet moans, dovelike sighs,
Chase not slumber from thy eyes.
Sweet moans, sweeter smiles,
All the dovelike moans beguiles.

Sweet babe, in thy face
Holy image I can trace.
Sweet babe once like thee,
Thy Maker lay and wept for me,

Wept for me, for thee, for all,
When He was an infant small.
Thou His image ever see,
Heavenly face that smiles on thee,

Smiles on thee, on me, on all;
Who became an infant small.
Infant smiles are His own smiles;
Heaven and Earth to peace beguiles.

WILLIAM BLAKE

You see this Christmas tree all silver gold?
It stood out many winters in the cold,
With tinsel sometimes made of crystal ice,
say once a winter morning–maybe twice.

More often it was trimmed by fallen snow
so heavy that the branches bent, with no
one anywhere to see how wondrous is
the hand of God in that white world of His.

And if you think it lonely through the night
when Christmas trees in houses take the light,
remember how His hand put up one star
in this same sky so long ago afar.

All stars are hung so every Christmas tree
has one above it. Let's go out and see.

DAVID McCORD

We have seen his star in the east,
and are come to worship him.
MATTHEW 2:2

"Oh, Lord, I thank You for the privilege and gift of living in a world filled with beauty and excitement and variety.

"I thank You for the gift of loving and being loved, for the friendliness and understanding and beauty of the animals on the farm and in the forest and marshes, for the green of the trees, the sound of a waterfall, the darting beauty of the trout in the brook.

"I thank You for the delights of music and children, of other men's thoughts and conversation and their books to read by the fireside or in bed with the rain falling on the roof or the snow blowing past outside the window."

LOUIS BROMFIELD

Christmas Eve, and twelve of the clock.
"Now they are all on their knees,"
An elder said, as we sat in a flock,
By the embers in fireside ease.

We pictured the meek mild creatures, where
They dwelt in their strawy pen,
Nor did it occur to one of us there
To doubt they were kneeling then.

So fair a fancy few would weave
In these years! Yet, I feel
If someone said, on Christmas Eve,
"Come; see the oxen kneel

"In the lonely barton by yonder comb,
Our childhood used to know,"
I should go with him in the gloom,
Hoping it might be so.

THOMAS HARDY

Goodman Joseph toiled through the snow—
Saw the star o'er a stable low;
Mary she might not further go—
Welcome thatch, and little below!
Joy was hers in the morning!

And then they heard the angels tell
Who were the first to cry Nowell?
Animals all, as it befell,
In the stable where they did dwell!
Joy shall be theirs in the morning!

KENNETH GRAHAME

His place of birth a solemn angel tells
To simple shepherds
keeping watch by night;
They gladly thither haste, and by a quire
Of squadroned angels hear His carol sung.

JOHN MILTON
FROM *Paradise Lost*

The time draws near the birth of Christ:
The moon is hid; the night is still;
The Christmas bells from hill to hill
Answer each other in the mist.

Four voices of four hamlets round,
From far and near, on mead and moor,
Swell out and fail, as if a door
Were shut between me and the sound:

Each voice four changes on the wind,
That now dilate, and now decrease,
Peace and good will, good will and peace,
Peace and good will, to all mankind.

ALFRED, LORD TENNYSON

Carol of the Russian Children

Snowbound mountains,
Snowbound valleys,
Snowbound plateaus, clad in white.
Fur-robed moujiks, fur-robed nobles,
Fur-robed children, see the light.

Shaggy pony, shaggy oxen,
Gentle shepherds wait the light;
Little Jesu, little mother,
Good St. Joseph, come this night.
Light! Light! Light!

ANONYMOUS

It is the calm and solemn night!
A thousand bells ring out and throw
Their joyous peals abroad, and smile
The darkness, charm'd and holy now!
The night that erst no name had worn,
To it a happy name is given
For in that stable lay new-born
The peaceful Prince of Earth and Heaven,
In the solemn midnight
Centuries ago.

ALFRED DOMETT

How simple we must grow!
How simple they who came!
The shepherds looked at God
Long before any man.
He sees God nevermore
Not there,
nor here on Earth
Who does not
long within
To be a
shepherd first.

ANGELUS SILESIUS,
FROM *Paradox*

Bright was the guiding star that led,
With mild, benignant ray,
The Gentiles to the lowly shed,
Where the Redeemer lay.

But lo! a brighter, clearer, light
Now points to His abode;
It shines, through sin and sorrow's night,
To guide us to our God.

Oh! haste to follow where it leads
The gracious call obey;
Be rugged wilds, or flowery meads,
The Christian's destined way.

Oh! gladly tread the narrow path,
While light and grace are given;
Who meekly follow Christ on Earth
Shall reign with Him in heaven.

HARRIET AUBER

Silent night! Holy night!
Shepherds quake at the sight!
Glories stream from heaven afar,
Heav'nly hosts sing Alleluia,
Christ, the Saviour, is born!
Christ, the Saviour, is born!

JOSEF MOHR

Born a King on Bethlehem's plain,
Gold I bring to crown Him again,
King forever, Ceasing never
Over us all to reign.

JOHN HENRY HOPKINS, JR.

The snow did come again, making their slow progress even slower. It was late on Christmas Eve, close to midnight, when the tired horses plodded up to the convent door. But lamps still burned. Manuela flew down the steps, Sister Francis Louise close behind her. And chilled and weary though she was, Mother Magdalene sensed instantly an excitement, an electricity in the air that she could not understand.

Nor did she understand it when they led her, still in her heavy wraps, down the corridor, into the new, as-yet-unused chapel where a few candles burned. "Look, Reverend Mother," breathed Sister Francis Louise. "Look!"

Like a curl of smoke the staircase rose before them, as insubstantial as a dream. Its top rested against the choir loft. Nothing else supported it; it seemed to float on air. Two complete spirals it made, the polished wood gleaming softly in the candlelight. "Thirty-three steps," whispered Sister Francis Louise. "One for each year in the life of Our Lord."

Mother Magdalene moved forward like a woman in a trance. She put her foot on the first step, then the second, then the third. There was not a tremor. She looked down, bewildered, at Manuela's ecstatic, upturned face. "But it's impossible! There wasn't time!"

"[The carpenter] finished yesterday," the sister said. "He didn't come today. No one has seen him anywhere in Sante Fe. He's gone."

"But who was he? Don't you even know his name?"

The Sister shook her head, but now Manuela pushed forward, nodding emphatically. "Jose!"

. . .Mother Magdalene felt her heart contract. Jose—the Spanish word for Joseph. Joseph the carpenter. Joseph the master wood-worker of. . .

"Jose!" Manuela's dark eyes were full of tears. "Jose!"

Silence, then, in the shadowy chapel. No one moved. Far away across the snow-silvered town Mother Magdalene heard a bell tolling midnight. . . . She felt uplifted by a great surge of wonder and gratitude and compassion and love. And she knew what it was. It was the spirit of Christmas. And it was upon them all.

ARTHUR GORDON,
"The Miraculous Staircase"

Suddenly a sound of music poured out into the bright air and drifted into the chamber. It was the boy choir singing Christmas anthems. Higher and higher rose the clear, fresh voices, full of hope and cheer, as children's voices always are. Fuller and fuller grew the burst of melody as one glad strain fell upon another in joyful harmony. . . .

KATE DOUGLAS WIGGIN,
"The Birds' Christmas Carol"

Joy to the world! The Saviour reigns;
Let men their songs employ;
While fields and floods, rocks, hills
   and plains
Repeat the sounding joy,
Repeat the sounding joy,
Repeat, repeat the sounding joy.

ISAAC WATTS

This star drew nigh unto the northwest;
O'er Bethlehem it took its rest,
And there it did both stop and stay,
Right over the place where Jesus lay:

Then entered in those wise men three,
Fell reverently upon their knee,
And offered there, in his presence,
Their gold and myrrh and frankincense:

Then let us all with one accord
Sing praises to our heavenly Lord,
That hath made heaven and Earth of nought,
And with His blood mankind hath bought.

TRADITIONAL ENGLISH CAROL

Shepherds, why this jubilee?
Why your joyful strains prolong?
What the gladsome tidings be
Which inspire your heav'nly song?
Come to Bethlehem and see
Him whose birth the angels sing;
Come adore on bended knee
Christ, the Lord, the new-born King.

TRADITIONAL FRENCH CAROL

Rise, shepherds, though the night is deep,
Rise from your slumber's dreaming!
Jesus, the shepherd, watch does keep,
In love all men redeeming.
Hasten to Mary, and look for her Child,
Come, shepherds, and greet our Savior mild!

AUSTRIAN SHEPHERD'S SONG

How silently, how silently,
The wondrous gift is giv'n!
So God imparts to
    human hearts
The blessing of His heav'n.
No ear may hear
    His coming,
But in this world of sin,
    Where meek souls will
    receive
        Him still,
    The dear Christ
        enters in.

PHILLIPS BROOKS

The little girl slept very heavily, and she slept very late, but she was wakened at last by the other children dancing 'round her bed with their stockings full of presents in their hands.

"What is it?" asked the little girl, and she rubbed her eyes and tried to rise up in bed.

"Christmas! Christmas! Christmas!" they all shouted, and waved their stockings.

WILLIAM DEAN HOWELLS,
"Christmas Every Day"

I heard the bells on Christmas Day
Their old, familiar carols play.
And wild and sweet
The words repeat
Of peace on Earth, good will to men!
HENRY WADSWORTH LONGFELLOW

Why do bells for Christmas ring?
Why do little children sing?

Once a lovely shining star,
Seen by shepherds from afar,
Gently moved until its light
Made a manger's cradle bright.

There a darling baby lay,
Pillowed soft upon the hay;
And its mother sang and smiled,
"This is Christ, the holy child!"

Therefore bells for Christmas ring,
Therefore little children sing.

TRADITIONAL SONG

B ells were ringing so merrily that it was hard to keep from dancing. Green garlands hung on the walls, and every tree was a Christmas tree full of toys, and blazing with candles that never went out. . . .

"Please tell me what splendid place this is," said Effie, as soon as she could collect her wits after the first look at all these astonishing things.

"This is the Christmas world; and here we work all the year round, never tired of getting ready for the happy day. . . ."

LOUISA MAY ALCOTT,
"A Christmas Dream and How It Came True"

Though I speak with the tongues of men and of angels,
and have not love, I am become as sounding brass or a tinkling cymbal.
And though I have the gift of prophecy, and understand
all mysteries, and all knowledge; and though I have all faith,
so that I could move mountains, and have not love, I am nothing.
1 CORINTHIANS 13:1–2

The stormy air was full of the sound of Christmas merriment as I walked from the streetcar to my small apartment. Bells rang and children shouted in the bitter dusk of the evening, and windows were lighted and everyone was running and laughing. But there would be no Christmas for me, I knew, no gifts, no remembrance whatsoever.

As I struggled through the snowdrifts, I just about reached the lowest point in my life. Unless a miracle happened I would be homeless in January, foodless, jobless. I had prayed steadily for weeks, and there had been no answer but this coldness and darkness, this harsh air, this abandonment.

. . .I went up three dusty flights of stairs, and I cried, shivering in my thin coat. But I made myself smile so I could greet my little daughter with a pretense of happiness. She opened the door for me and threw herself in my arms, screaming joyously and demanding that we decorate the tree immediately. . . .

I stood in the cold little kitchen, and misery overwhelmed me. For the first time in my life, I doubted the existence of God and His mercy, and the coldness in my heart was colder than ice.

The doorbell rang, and Peggy ran fleetly to answer it, calling that it must be Santa Claus. Then I heard a man talking heartily to her and went to the door. He was a delivery man, and his arms were full of big parcels, and he was laughing at my child's frenzied joy and her dancing. "This is a mistake," I said, but he read the name on the parcels, and they were for me. When he had gone I could only stare at the boxes.

TAYLOR CALDWELL,
"My Christmas Miracle"

There is one glory of the sun,
and another glory of the moon,
and another glory of the stars:
for the one star differeth
from another star in glory.
1 CORINTHIANS 15:41

Josh looked again at the woman and the child, then limped across the stable. He stopped next to the mother and looked into the baby's face. The baby was crying. He was cold. The woman picked up the baby and put him on the hay next to her.

Josh looked around the stable for something to keep the baby warm. Usually there were blankets. But not tonight. The shepherds had taken them on their trip across the valley.

Then Josh remembered his own soft, warm wool. Timidly, he walked over and curled up close to the baby.

"Thank you, little lamb," the baby's mother said softly.

Soon the little child stopped crying and went back to sleep.

About that time, a man entered the stable carrying some rags.

"I'm sorry, Mary," he explained. "This is all the cover I could find."

"It's okay," she answered. "This little lamb has kept the new King warm."

A King? Joshua looked at the baby and wondered who he might be.

"His name is Jesus." Mary spoke as if she knew Josh's question. "God's Son. He came from heaven to teach us about God."

MAX LUCADO,
The Crippled Lamb

What Child is this who, laid to rest
On Mary's lap is sleeping?
Whom angels greet with anthems sweet,
While shepherds watch are keeping?
This, this is Christ the King,
Whom shepherds guard and angels sing;
Haste, haste, to bring Him laud,
The Babe, the Son of Mary.

WILLIAM CHATTERTON DIX

LOVE AND JOY

O righteous Father,
You have showered us
with Your love and joy.
And the gift of Yourself
surpasses any other
that we might receive
in our earthly travels.
Keep me ever mindful,
ever grateful for Your love.
Amen.

> He loves each one of us,
> as if there were only one of us.
> ST. AUGUSTINE

The magi, as you know, were wise men, wonderful wise men, who brought gifts to the Babe in the manger. They invented the art of giving Christmas presents. Being wise, their gifts were no doubt wise ones, possibly bearing the privilege of exchange in case of duplication. And here I have lamely related to you the uneventful chronicle of two foolish children in a flat who most unwisely sacrificed for each other the greatest treasures of their house. But in a last word to the wise of these days let it be said that of all who give gifts these two were the wisest. Of all who give and receive gifts, such as they are wisest. Everywhere they are wisest. They are the magi.

O. HENRY,
"The Gift of the Magi"

We miss the spirit of Christmas if we consider the incarnation as an indistinct and doubtful, far-off event unrelated to our present problems. We miss the purport of Christ's birth if we do not accept it as a living link which joins us together in spirit as children of the ever-living and true God. In love alone—the love of God and the love of man—will be found the solution of all the ills which afflict the world today. Slowly, sometimes painfully, but always with increasing purpose, emerges the great message of Christianity: Only with wisdom comes joy, and with greatness comes love.

HARRY S. TRUMAN

Jesus is God spelling Himself
out in language that
man can understand.
S. D. GORDON

Some say that ever again
that season comes wherein
Our Saviour's birth is celebrated
the bird of dawning
singeth all night long.
. . .So hallowed and so
gracious is the time.

WILLIAM SHAKESPEARE,
Hamlet

Christmas Day declares that He dwelt among us. . . . This is the festival which makes us know, indeed, that we are members of one body; it binds together the life of Christ on Earth with His life in heaven; it assures us that Christmas Day belongs not to time but to eternity.

FREDERICK DENISON MAURICE

There is an inescapable logic in the Christmas message:
we experience joy, quite simply, in self-surrender,
in giving up our lives. Joy calls for renunciation.

LADISLAUS BOROS

If gaily clothed and proudly fed
In dangerous wealth we dwell,
Remind us of Thy manger bed
And lowly cottage cell.

If pressed by poverty severe
In anxious want we pine,
O may Thy Spirit whisper near
How poor a lot was Thine!

Through this life's ever varying scene
From sin preserve us free;
Like us Thou hast a mourner been,
May we rejoice with Thee!

REGINALD HEBER

The ox and the ass
understood more of the
first Christmas than the
high priests in Jerusalem.
And it is the same today.
THOMAS MERTON

This Prince, do they desire to find Him?
They're worn out swaddling clothes that bind Him.
A manger, spread with hay's His bed.
His throne is higher than the highest,
Yet He among the cattle lieth;
What Him to such a lot has led?

HENRICUS SELYNS

"Christmas won't be Christmas without any presents," grumbled Jo, lying on the rug.

"It's so dreadful to be poor!" sighed Meg, looking down at her old dress.

"I don't think it's fair for some girls to have lots of pretty things, and other girls nothing at all," added little Amy with an injured sniff.

"We've got Father and Mother and each other," said Beth contentedly from her corner.

LOUISA MAY ALCOTT,
Little Women

> Calm on the listening ear of night
> Come heaven's melodious strains,
> Where wild Judaea stretches far
> Her silver-mantled plains.

EDMUND H. SEARS

" 'I have often thought,'
said Sir Roger,
'it happens very well
that Christmas should fall out
in the middle of winter.' "
JOSEPH ADDISON

At Christmas I no more desire a rose
Than wish a snow in May's new-fangled mirth;
But like of each thing that in season grows.

WILLIAM SHAKESPEARE,
Love's Labour's Lost

HOPE
AND A
FUTURE

Dear heavenly Father,
You delight in giving.
You gave us the gift of Your Son—
and because of Jesus, we have the
gifts of new life and life eternal.
Thank You, Lord, now and forever.

In the course of justice none of us
Should see salvation: We do pray for mercy.
WILLIAM SHAKESPEARE

Break forth, O beauteous heavenly light,
And usher in the morning;
O shepherds, shrink not with afright,
But hear the angel's warning.
This Child, now weak in infancy,
Our confidence and joy shall be,
The power of Satan breaking,
Our peace eternal making.

JOHANN RIST

Therefore if any man be in Christ, he is a new creature:
old things are passed away; behold, all things are become new.
2 CORINTHIANS 5:17

Dear Christian people all, rejoice,
Each soul with joy upraising.
Pour forth a song with heart and voice,
With love and gladness singing.
Give thanks to God, our Lord above,
Thanks for His miracle of love!
Dearly He hath redeemed us.

He spoke to His belovèd Son
With infinite compassion:
"Go hence, my heart's most precious One,
Be to the lost Salvation;
Death, his relentless tyrant, stay,
And bear him from his sins away
With Thee to live forever!"

MARTIN LUTHER

Hallo!" growled Scrooge, in his accustomed voice, as near as he could feign it. "What do you mean by coming here at this time of day?"

"I am very sorry, sir. I am behind my time."

"You are? Yes. I think you are. Step this way if you please."

"It's only once a year, sir. It shall not be repeated. I was making rather merry yesterday, sir."

"Now, I'll tell you what, my friend. I am not going to stand this sort of thing any longer. And therefore," Scrooge continued, leaping from his stool, and giving Bob such a dig in the waistcoat that he staggered back into the tank again, "and therefore I am about to raise your salary!"

Bob trembled and got a little nearer to the ruler.

"A merry Christmas, Bob!" said Scrooge, with an earnestness that could not be mistaken, as he clapped him on the back. "A merrier Christmas, Bob, my good fellow, than I have given you for many a year! I'll raise your salary, and endeavor to assist your struggling family, and we will discuss your affairs this very afternoon, over a Christmas bowl of smoking bishop, Bob! Make up the fires, and buy a second coal-scuttle before you dot another *i*, Bob Cratchitt!"

CHARLES DICKENS,
A Christmas Carol

For God so loved the world,
that he gave his only begotten Son,
that whosoever believeth in him should not perish,
but have everlasting life.
JOHN 3:16

True love's the gift
which God has given
To man alone
beneath the heaven.
SIR WALTER SCOTT

And all things are of God, who hath reconciled us
to himself by Jesus Christ.
2 CORINTHIANS 5:18

I have learned that human existence is essentially tragic. It is only the love of God, disclosed and enacted in Christ, that redeems the human tragedy and makes it tolerable. No, more than tolerable. Wonderful.

ANGUS DUN

Knowing this, that the trying
of your faith worketh patience.
But let patience have her perfect work,
that ye may be perfect and entire,
wanting nothing.

JAMES 1:3–4

Now let us thank the Eternal Power: convinced
That heaven but tries our virtue by affliction;
That oft the cloud which wraps the present hour
Serves but to brighten all our future days.

JOHN BROWN

Good King Wenceslas looked out on the Feast of Stephen,
When the snow lay round about, deep and crisp and even.
Brightly shone the moon that night, though the frost was cruel,
When a poor man came in sight, gathering winter fuel.

"Hither, page, and stand by me, if you know it, telling,
Yonder peasant, who is he? Where and what his dwelling?"
"Sire, he lives a good league hence, underneath the mountain,
Right against the forest fence, by Saint Agnes' fountain."

"Bring me food and bring me wine, bring me pine logs hither,
You and I will see him dine, when we bear them thither."
Page and monarch, forth they went, forth they went together,
Through the cold wind's wild lament and the bitter weather.

JOHN MASON NEALE

U_p, far as the men could see, there was flashing of white wings, and coming and going of radiant forms, and voices as of a multitude chanting in unison.

"Glory to God in the highest, and on Earth peace, good will toward men!"

Not once the praise, but many times.

Then the herald raised his eyes as seeking approval of one far off; his wings stirred, and spread slowly and majestically, on their upper side as snow, in the shadow vari-tinted, like mother-of-pearl; when the were expanded many cubits beyond his stature, he rose lightly, and, without effort, floated out of view, taking the light up with him. Long after he was gone, down from the sky fell the refrain in measure mellowed by distance, "Glory to God in the highest, and on Earth peace, good will toward men."

When the shepherds came fully to their senses, they stared at each stupidly, until one of them said, "It was Gabriel, the Lord's messenger unto men."

None answered.

Then another recovered his voice, and replied, "That is what he said."

"And did he not also say, in the city of David, which is our Bethlehem yonder. And that we should find him a babe in swaddling clothes?"

"And lying in a manger."

The first speaker gazed into the fire thoughtfully, but at length said, like one possessed of a sudden resolve, "There is but one place in Bethlehem where there are mangers; but one, and that is in the cave near the old khan. Brethren, let us go see this thing which has come to pass. The priests and doctors have been a long time looking for the Christ. Now He is born, and the Lord has given us a sign by which to know Him. Let us go up and worship Him."

LEW WALLACE,
Ben-Hur

I know not how that Bethlehem's Babe
Could in the Godhead be;
I only know the manger Child
Has brought God's life to me.

I know not how that Calvary's cross
A world from sin could free;
I only know its matchless love
Has brought God's love to me.

I know not how that Joseph's tomb
Could solve death's mystery;
I only know a living Christ,
Our immortality.

HARRY WEBB FARRINGTON

We Christians may rejoice today
When Christ was born to comfort and to save us.
Who thus believes no longer grieves,
For none are lost who grasp the hope He gave us.

The hither throng with happy song
To Him whose birth and death are our assurance;
Through whom are we at last set free
From sins and burdens that surpassed endurance.

Yea, let us praise Our God and raise
Loud hallelujahs to the skies above us.
The bliss bestowed today by God
To ceaseless thankfulness and joy should move us.

CASPAR FÜGER,
TRANSLATED BY CATHERINE WINKWORTH

For unto us a child is born, unto us a son is given:
and the government shall be upon his shoulder:
and his name shall be called Wonderful, Counsellor, The mighty God,
The everlasting Father, The Prince of Peace.

ISAIAH 9:6

Jesus answered and said unto him,
Verily, verily, I say unto thee,
Except a man be born again,
he cannot see the kingdom of God.

JOHN 3:3

Have I allowed my personal human life to become a "Bethlehem" for the Son of God? I cannot enter into the realm of the Kingdom of God unless I am born from above by a birth totally unlike natural birth. "Ye must be born again."

OSWALD CHAMBERS

Good Christian men, rejoice with heart and soul, and voice;
Give ye heed to what we say:
News! News! Jesus Christ is born today;
Ox and ass before Him bow; and He is in the manger now.
Christ is born today! Christ is born today!

Good Christian men, rejoice, with heart and soul and voice;
Now ye hear of endless bliss: Joy! Joy!
Jesus Christ was born for this!
He has opened the heavenly door,
    and man is blest forevermore.
Christ was born for this! Christ was born for this!

Good Christian men, rejoice, with heart and soul and voice;
Now ye need not fear the grave: Peace! Peace!
Jesus Christ was born to save!
Calls you one and calls you all, to gain His everlasting hall.
Christ was born to save! Christ was born to save!

HEINRICH SUSO,
TRANSLATED BY JOHN MASON NEALE

And the
shepherds returned,
glorifying and praising God
for all the things
that they had heard
and seen.
LUKE 2:20

Joy to the world, the Lord is come!
Let Earth receive her King;
Let every heart prepare Him room,
And heaven and nature sing,
And heaven and nature sing,
And heaven, and heaven, and nature sing.

No more let sins and sorrows grow,
Nor thorns infest the ground;
He comes to make His blessings flow
Far as the curse is found,
Far as the curse is found,
Far as, far as, the curse is found.

He rules the world with truth and grace,
And makes the nations prove
The glories of His righteousness,
And wonders of His love,
And wonders of His love,
And wonders, wonders, of His love.

ISAAC WATTS

Oh, Lord, grant that this
Christmas season
will be a celebration of You.
We rejoice in the Father
Who sent His only Son.
We rejoice in the Son,
Who came as a Baby in a manger.
We rejoice in the Spirit that lives
in the hearts of those who believe.
May we give our lives to You,
as You have to us. Amen.

Compact Disc Track Selections

1. We Three Kings–Jazz Piano (2:22)[1]
2. Hark! the Herald Angels Sing–Saxophone (2:58)[1]
3. Angels We Have Heard on High–Gospel Choir (3:38)[1]
4. Go, Tell It on the Mountain–Kid's Sing-Along (2:37)[2]
5. It Came Upon the Midnight Clear–Classical Guitar (1:58)[1]
6. O Little Town of Bethlehem–Vocal Southern Gospel (4:15)[1]
7. O Come, O Come, Emmanuel–Harp & Strings (2:16)[1]
8. The First Noel–Vocal Southern Gospel (2:55)[1]
9. Away in a Manger–Classical Guitar (2:26)[1]
10. What Child Is This?–Kid's Sing-Along (3:08)[2]
11. Bring a Torch, Jeanette Isabella–Harp & Strings (2:43)[1]
12. Do You Hear What I Hear?–Piano (3:35)[3]
13. O Come, All Ye Faithful–Gospel Choir (3:31)[1]
14. The Little Drummer Boy–Saxophone (4:40)[1]

Copyright and Permissions
1 Tennessee Production Center
2 Nite Lite Ministries
3 Total Telemart, Inc.